THIS BOOK BELONGS TO

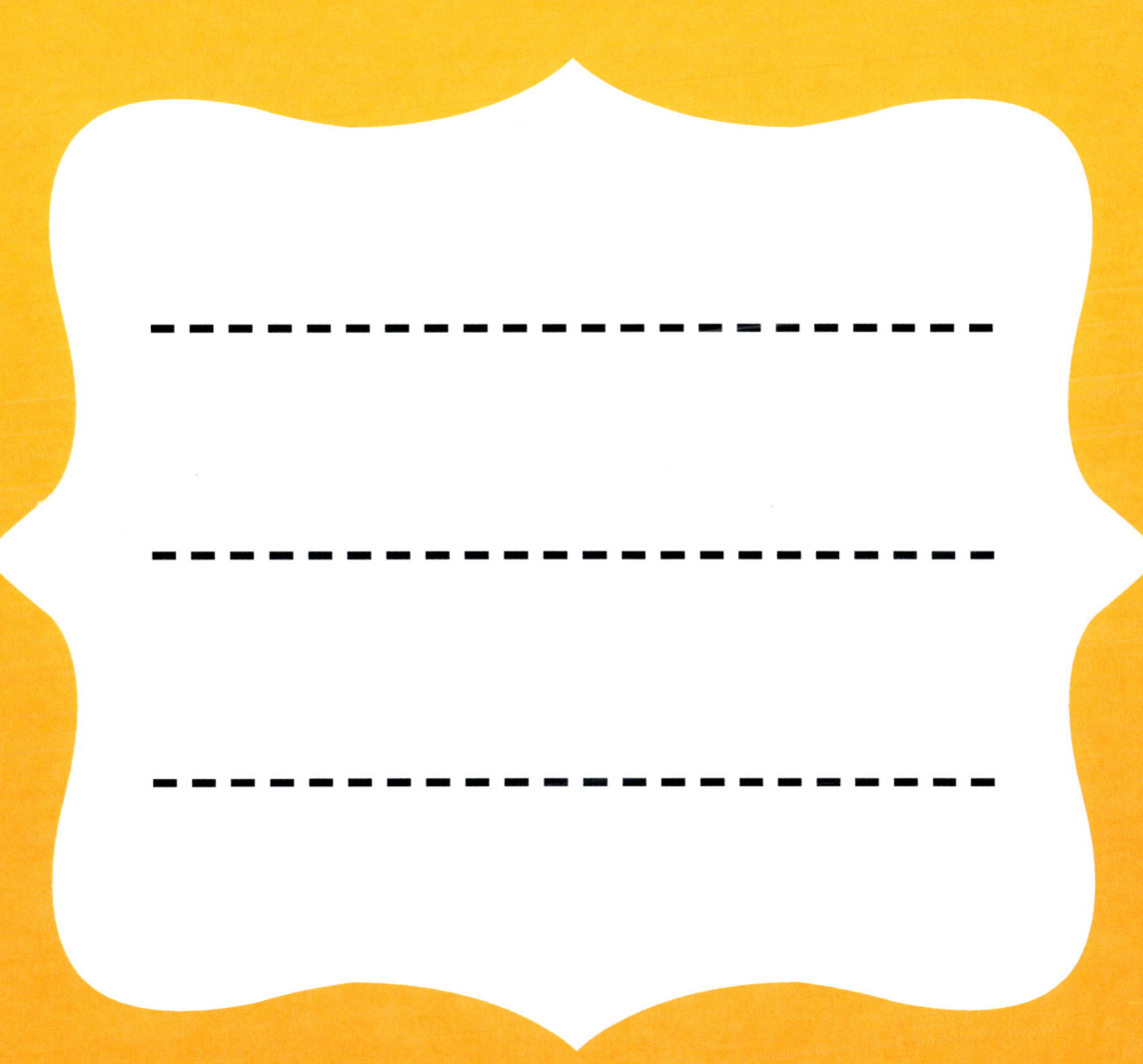

DIVERSED IN STEM

When We Believe, We Achieve

STEM PLUG

Diversed In Stem: When We Believe, We Achieve
All Rights Reserved
Text Copyright © 2022 Richard S. T Gilliam
STEM Logo Copyright © 2022 Richard S. T Gilliam
Image Copyright © 2022 Wealth Builders Network, Inc.

Published by Global Book Publishing
https://globalbookpublishing.com
ISBN: 978-1-956193-15-2

Global Book Publishing

This book is dedicated to my mother Sheila Gilliam for inspiring me throughout my life.

This book is also dedicated to anyone who has ever struggled with self-belief, just know that anything you vision can be created with self-determination.

WHAT IS STEM?

Intro — Did you know that STEM is involved in about all aspects of our lives?

STEM is much more than a group of disparate concepts bunched together. STEM is a teaching philosophy that integrates four important disciplines. STEM is the future, as it creates endless opportunities. With our world growing and changing every day, STEM is what shapes all good things to come. Being exposed to science, technology, engineering, and math is important for building knowledge in young minds.

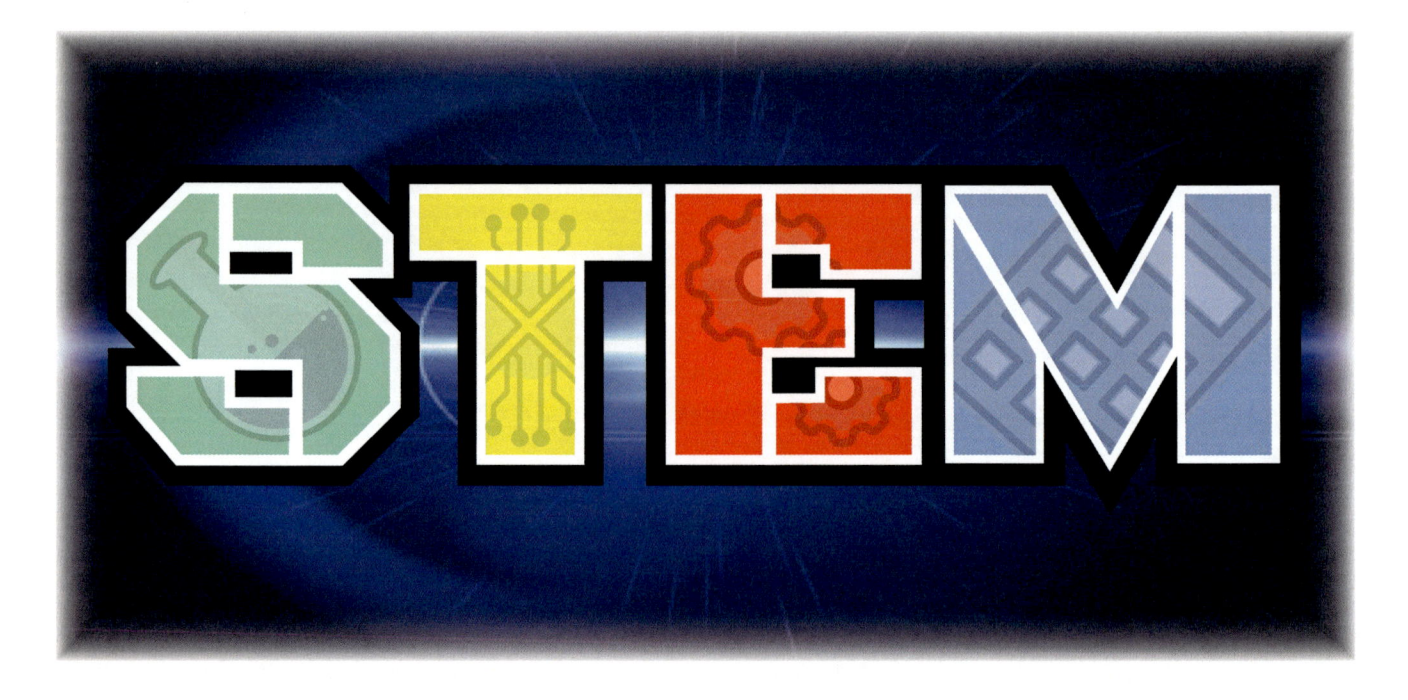

Science is everywhere around us. It's the study of life.

Technology will be continuing to expand in every way in the future.

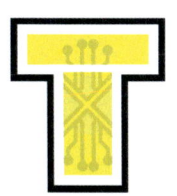

Engineering deals with the design work of some of our important infrastructures such as roads and bridges.

Math is all around us and a part of everything that we do. Math can be thought of as the central building block in our lives.

Now that we know more about exactly what STEM is and what it can do, let's look at our character personalities and how these qualities can determine how best to excel in STEM-related careers.

PERSONALITIES

Intro — Did you know everyone is born with a distinct personality type and unique characteristics?

The goal of this is book is to demonstrate that some of our children's personality traits that we deem negative can wind up being positive, leading to a great outcome for the future.

All the characters in this book belong to the same class and are highly unique yet interconnected—as you soon shall see!

The fifth-grade class at Garvey Middle School is taught by Ms. Joy, who is from Ghana. Diverse though the students are, their brains and ways of thinking share much in common. This chapter will show you that no matter the background in question, kids can dream big . . . if they're equipped with self-knowledge.

STEM fields affect almost every aspect of our lives. Great new inventions in STEM come from individuals working together and problem-solving, seeking out solutions. Having diverse minds and backgrounds can greatly benefit these events.

But why is increasing STEM diversity so complicated?

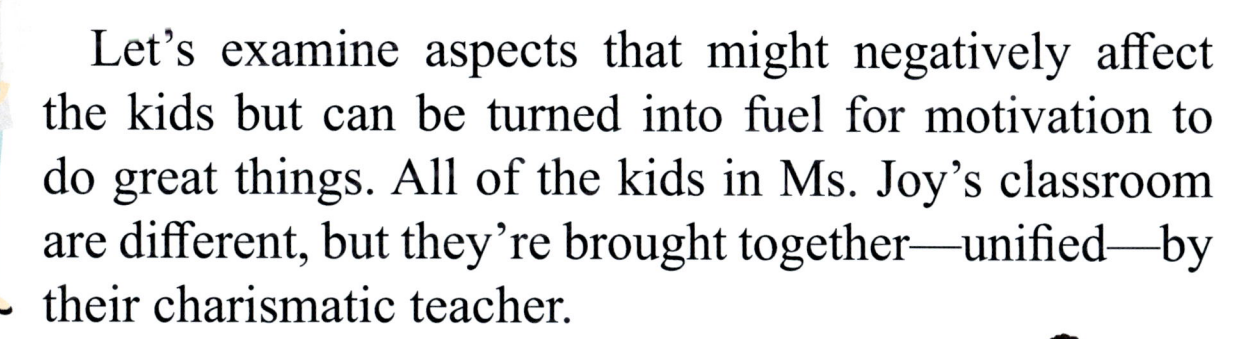

Let's examine aspects that might negatively affect the kids but can be turned into fuel for motivation to do great things. All of the kids in Ms. Joy's classroom are different, but they're brought together—unified—by their charismatic teacher.

Ms. Joy has asked each student to grab a partner and discuss each other's family backgrounds. Ms. Joy's goal is to show the kids that even though they're from diverse backgrounds, they all can do great things. "Class, partner up," she says. "This exercise will show us our differences, and we'll be able to learn a great deal from each other. I want us to discuss a problem that we sometimes deal with that may be holding us back. Please be respectful to your partner, considering what they have to share."

Dommingo, Iaan, Victoria, Eia, Richie, Saanvi, Emily, Danny, Ichiro, and Nina get fast to work!

Dommingo is a Spanish boy. He's a very shy boy, but he loves to draw. Dommingo struggles with confidence but draws to make himself feel better. One of the reasons that Dommingo struggles with confidence is because he is repeating the grade, so he doesn't feel smart or good enough.

Dommingo lives with his Dad and his little sister, Nina, who is also in his class. Dommingo's mother passed away, which has also affected his confidence.

Dommingo's mother used to always tell him how proud she was of him. But since she has been gone, Dommingo has lost his confidence. He draws because his mother was an artist and he feels that he connects with his mother when he draws. Dommingo feels that his mother connects with him through his drawings.

Iaan is an Indian boy. He's a very friendly boy that loves to help his classmates. He loves to help when others are in need. He has a lot of compassion and patience for others.

Iaan has recently moved to America from India. His parents sent him to America to live with his uncle. Iaan's father's brother suggested that Iaan lives with him. Iaan is very appreciative to live in America, so that's why he proves so helpful. Iaan's friendliness is rooted in his having come from him coming from another country and wanting to fit in with the other kids.

Victoria is an African American girl who loves to organize things. As a young girl, she is very organized and passionate about the work she does. Victoria can be very blunt at times.

Victoria lives with her mother and her father. She has a big sister that has just gone away to college. Victoria's big sister's personality has had a big effect on her. Victoria pays a lot of attention to her big sister's actions and wants to be like her.

"I want to be like her"

Eia is an Asian girl who is very quiet but very focused. She is very realistic and likes to work independently. She is a very neat little girl. Eia can be standoffish at times when dealing with her classmates.

Eia lives with her mother and father. Eia's father puts a lot of pressure on her to do well even in the fifth grade. He tells Eia what she has to be when she grows up too. Eia has a cat named Bonnie that she loves and talks to. She feels that Bonnie is the only one who doesn't put pressure on her.

Richie is an African American boy. Though he's a slow learner and it takes him long to learn certain processes, he is very creative. Richie does, at times, feel he's not good enough to do certain things, but even so, he never gives up. He thinks outside the box and loves creating things. He is a very persistent and adaptable child. Richie gets along with everyone, no matter what background they come from. Richie can make impulsive decisions at times.

Richie lives with his mother and is an only child. He spends summers with his father, who lives in a different state. Richie's parents are divorced. Richie has an imaginary friend that he calls his sibling who helps him bring out his creativity. Richie's love for creating things comes from wanting to make his mother proud. Richie's motivation to never give up even when it takes him a while to learn something comes from his mother.

Saanvi is an Indian American girl that is very adventurous. She is very mature for her age and is incredibly passionate. At times, Saanvi's can be somewhat outrageous.

Saanvi lives with her mom and dad. Saanvi's cousin is Iaan. Saanvi gets her adventurous nature from her mother, who goes on hikes with her a lot. Saanvi's dad thinks that she is too adventurous for her age but realizes she got it from her mom.

Emily is a Caucasian girl that loves to read. She is very quiet and keeps to herself. Emily is considered a Tomboy—the opposite of a girly girl. Emily doubts herself at times because she doesn't look like the typical girl.

Emily lives with her mother, father, and two brothers. Emily doesn't see her father a lot because he is always working. She looks up to her two older brothers, which is the reason she can come off as tomboyish. Deep down, Emily misses spending time with her father, who is always working, which is one of the reasons she is always quiet and keeps to herself.

Ichiro is an Asian boy who is very generous. He is also very humorous and likes to make his classmates laugh. Ichiro can sometimes say some bizarre things in class.

Ichiro currently lives with his grandmother, who he helps look after. Ichiro's parents are around, but he wanted to live with his grandmother to look after her. Ichiro's generosity comes from his grandmother and how he knows to care for her.

Danny is a Caucasian boy who loves to build. He is a daring child that likes to take on challenges and is very competitive in all that he does. Danny can be very anxious at times, ever seeking to get things his way. Danny's anxiety causes him to get mad if he doesn't get his way, and this often affects him negatively.

Danny lives with his mother, father, and his older brother. Danny's older brother picks on him at home, which makes Danny very competitive at things at school with her other kids. Danny gets his love of building because his dad is an architect.

"Leave me alone!"

Nina is a Spanish girl who is very energetic and competitive. Nina's competitiveness sometimes intimidates those around her. This makes Nina sad because deep down inside, she doesn't mean any harm.

Nina lives with her father and brother, Dommingo. Nina's mother has passed away. Her competitive spirit comes from her being the little sister who wants to outshine her big brother.

STEM CAREERS

Intro | Did you know STEM jobs are expected to grow by 8% this decade alone?

Ms. Joy is in high spirits as always. "Okay, class! So, today our assignment is to discuss personality traits we feel that we all have. Today, I'll go around the room and let everyone share a personality trait. After the last person is done sharing a trait, I want everyone to close your eyes and imagine yourselves in one of the cool STEM careers we discussed. By the time you all grow up—big and strong—there will be so many fun things you can spend your life doing. The goal is for us to use our imagination and bring it to life. Okay, class?

"Let's start with you, Dommingo. What trait do you have?"

Dommingo: "Well, I love to draw. That's all I can really think of, Ms. Joy."

Ms. Joy: "Dommingo, you're very creative, and your drawings are amazing."

Hearing this, Dommingo imagines himself as an architect. With Dommingo's creative mind, he would make a great architect! As an architect, introverted Dommingo could use the same tactics that he currently uses for his drawings in class.

Ms. Joy: "Okay, Iaan. What traits do you have?"

Iaan: "I think I'm a good listener."

Ms. Joy: "Iaan, you are a great listener, and that's a great quality to have! It will certainly help you strive in your STEM career."

Complimented as such, Iaan imagines himself as a psychiatrist. One of the most important qualities of a psychiatrist is empathy. With Iaan's great listening and observation skills, he sees this as a perfect career.

Ms. Joy: "Okay, Victoria. What trait do you have?"

Victoria: "I think I'm very organized."

Ms. Joy: "Yes, you are, Victoria. Your organization skills will really help you excel too."

Now Victoria sees herself as a lab manager. She would make a great lab manager with all of the passion she has as a young girl. A lab manager is responsible for leading the function of a laboratory. Lab managers must be organized and equipped to make tough decisions.

Ms. Joy: "Okay, Eia. What trait do you have?"

Eia: "Well, Ms. Joy, I'm not really sure. I would say I'm very quiet. I do feel like I'm very neat and organized, though."

Ms. Joy: "Eia, there are multiple STEM careers that can make great use of your quiet nature."

Eia imagines herself as a medical writer. A medical writer is a perfect STEM career for a quiet person. Her neatness and organization would allow her to strive in such a career. As a medical writer, Eia will write scientific documents. Although she may be quiet her, career could still speak volumes.

"Well, Ms. Joy, I do think I'm pretty creative."

Ms. Joy: "I fully agree, Richie. You're very creative. Just imagine what that ability will allow you to do in a STEM career!"

Richie imagines himself as a robotic engineer. With Richie's creativity, a robotic engineer would make a perfect career for him. As a robotic engineer, creativity can go a long way. It's especially important when dealing with brand-new designs. Even as a slow learner, Richie's persistence will allow him to do anything he puts his mind to.

Ms. Joy: "Okay, Saanvi. What trait do you have?"

Saanvi: "Well, Ms. Joy, I feel as though I'm adventurous."

Ms. Joy: "Saanvi, that's great! Your love for the outdoors can lead you to a really fun STEM career."

Saanvi imagines herself as a zoologist. Saanvi's love for the outdoors will make her a great zoologist. Also, with her sense of adventure, she would work with some very big animals that others would find too intimidating. As a zoologist, she will study animals and their amazing abilities.

24

Ms. Joy: "Okay, Danny. What trait do you have?"

Danny: "Ms. Joy, I think I'm pretty competitive. I don't like losing—at all."

Ms. Joy: "Yes, Danny, you are very competitive but you can use that to your advantage in the career you seek."

Danny imagines himself as a toolmaker. As a toolmaker, Danny will work with different metals to make important tools. Danny's love to build and his competitiveness will help him with the precision involved in making tools.

Ms. Joy: "Okay, Emily. What trait do you have?"

Emily: "Well, Ms. Joy, I do like computers and playing with designs on them."

Ms. Joy: "That's amazing, Emily. Your wanting to design and use technology could lead you to something very fun."

Emily imagines herself as a web developer. As a web developer, she will play an important role in creating and maintaining websites.

"Well, Ms. Joy, I think I'm very generous."

Ms. Joy: "That's great Ichiro. This will help you excel when it comes to your career."

Ichiro imagines himself as a sports medicine physician. With Ichiro's personality, this would be a great career for him, as he would be well-equipped to treat athletes and make important decisions, determining if an athlete is fit to play after an injury.

Ms. Joy: "Okay, Nina, what trait do you have?"

Nina: "Well, Ms. Joy, I think I have a lot of energy, and I do like talking to people."

Ms. Joy: "That's great, Nina. Your energetic personality will help you strive in your STEM career."

Nina imagines herself as a pharmacist. With her energetic personality, she would excel working with patients. Her competitiveness would be an important quality while working in a busy environment and needing to get things done. Nina would show her patients how to use and store their medicine.

COLLABORATION

Intro: Did you know collaboration can help form deeper and creative thoughts towards a specific subject?

Big challenges are rarely solved by individuals. Working on STEM problems also involves learning to work as a productive part of a collaborative team. Let's see how the careers that the characters envision themselves in can actually lead to collaboration.

"Class," says Ms. Joy, "I wanted everyone to do this exercise to see how great—and possible—the things we see ourselves doing when we all align with one another. Even with our diverse backgrounds, we're able to put our thinking together to create success in STEM."

Ms. Joy begins to write on the board.

"Class I'm not sure if you realize this, but just from your thoughts and visions, you have set a blueprint for yourselves. It's just like we like to say: when we believe, we achieve."

"Now I'm going to explain how the careers you envisioned yourselves in actually lead to working together at times . . .

Dommingo, you as an architect—your ideas and designs will be important to Victoria as a manager of a lab space. Danny, the tools that you make will be needed to build that lab that Victoria will run. Emily, your career as a web developer will be important to Eia because you will be developing the sites that her medical writing will go on. Ichiro and Iaan, as a sports medicine physician and psychiatrist, you will work with Nina as a pharmacist to prescribe medicine to your patients. Saanvi, you as a zoologist might interact with Richie, a robotic engineer, to help design a robot for you that can help you study the habits of some of the animals in your studies.

So, no matter our different personalities, backgrounds, and colors, we all have valuable qualities."

EXPLORING STEM CAREERS

Intro: Did you know there are a variety of settings one can work in a STEM career?

There are many STEM careers one can explore. Here's a list of great STEM careers arranged and defined alphabetically. Listed with each STEM career are personality traits one might have.

Analytical Chemist: Determines the structure, composition, and nature of substances by examining and identifying their various elements or compounds.

Qualities: Logical mind, Numerical and Analytical ability

Beekeeper: Cares for bees and provides bees with hives for shelter and medication.

Qualities: Investigative, Curious

Civil Engineer: Plans, designs, and constructs roads, bridges, and similar dams.

Qualities: Communicative, Creative

Dietitian: Experts in the use of food and nutrition to promote health and manage diseases. They help to assess their client's needs and develop meal plans for them.

Qualities: Good Listener, Solution-oriented, Compassionate

Ecologist: Studies how plants and animals interact with society.

Qualities: Passion for nature, Solution-oriented

Food Scientist: Source for new nutritional food sources and investigate avenues for making processed foods safe, healthy, and taste good. They also find the best way to distribute, process, preserve and package the food.

Qualities: Attention to detail, Analytical and Communication skills

Geologist: Studies the materials of the earth such as solid, liquid, and gaseous materials.

Qualities: Passion for nature, Good analytical skills

Histotechnologist: Forms a part of the medical lab team that works with humans, animals, or plant samples to determine specific diagnoses. The main job of a histotechnologist is to prepare these samples for analysis.

Qualities: Solution-oriented, Reliable, and works well under pressure

Industrial Engineer: Finds ways to eliminate wastefulness in the production process. Industrial engineers can work in many different settings from health care to manufacturing. Their main goal is to make the industrial work environment as efficient as possible.

Qualities: Attentive, Independent mind

Java Developer: They are computer programmers who are efficient in programming in Java. Their responsibilities include implementation, designing, testing and resolving any technical issues that may occur during programming. Many big organizations use Java because it is less complex, making Java Developers well sought-after.

Qualities: Positive attitude, Curiosity, Communicative

Kinesiologist: Looks for ways to improve the performance of the human body. A kinesiologist recognizes the relationship of energies within the body with every muscle, tissue, and organ and is able to apply healing techniques for the body.

Qualities: Interpersonal skills, Analytical skills, Problem-solving skills

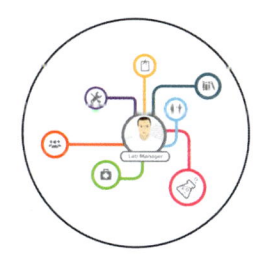

Lab Manager: Oversees the operations of a scientific laboratory. Lab managers make sure operations are running smoothly by scheduling lab staff, ordering supplies, and making sure everyone is following proper protocols.

Qualities: Solution-oriented, Collaborative, Organized

Medical Writer: Writes documentation that deals with medicine or health care.

Qualities: Self-motivated, Inquisitive

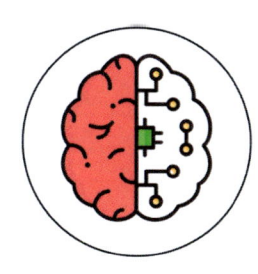

Neurologist: Medical doctor who diagnoses, treats, and manages diseases or infections of the brain and nervous system.

Qualities: Solution-oriented, Patience, Dexterity

Ophthalmologist: A doctor who specializes in eye and vision care. Ophthalmologists are also involved in scientific research on the causes and cures for eye diseases and vision disorders.

Qualities: Communicative, Empathetic, Hand-eye coordination

Pharmacist: Healthcare professionals who specialize in the right way to use, store, preserve, and provide medicine.

Qualities: Patience, Detail-oriented, Knowledgeable

Quality Scientist: Scientist who is responsible for performing an analysis of the goods and products from the manufacturing business related to medical or science industries. Ensures the quality of raw materials and resources used in production, inspects the features and specifications of the product, and also checks its adherence to high-quality standards and safe consumption.

Qualities: Curious, Detail-oriented, Critical thinking

Robotic Engineer: Designs and develops robotic equipment. Robotics engineers help to make jobs safer, easier, and more efficient.

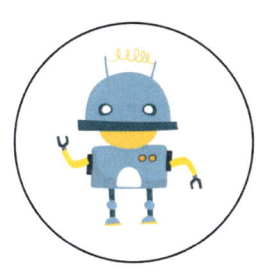

Qualities: Analytical and solution-oriented, Communicative, Problem Solver

Sports Medicine Physician: These are licensed health professionals who assist athletes and physically fit individuals with rehabilitation from musculoskeletal injuries. They diagnose, treat, and help prevent injuries that occur during sporting events, athletic training, and physical activities.

Qualities: Communicative, Decisive, Empathetic

Toolmaker: Makes precision tools, holding devices, and special guides that are used in the manufacturing process.

Qualities: Accurate, Attention to detail

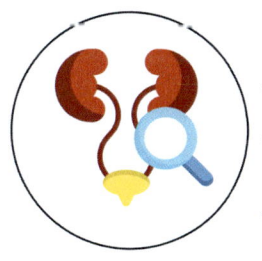

Urologist: These are medical doctors who treat the urinary system (kidneys, bladder, ureters) Urologists diagnose and treat diseases of the urinary tract in men and women.

Qualities: Empathetic, Adaptable

Veterinarian: Examines animals to assess their health and diagnose any problems. Promotes the health of animals by advising animal owners about sanitation measures, feeding, and general care.

Qualities: Compassionate, Interpersonal skills, Solution-oriented

Web Developer: Responsible for the coding, design, and layout of a website according to a company's specifications. Generally assists with the maintenance and upkeep of the website.

Qualities: Detailed, Computer literate, Creative

X-ray Technologist: Health care professional that specializes in using the equipment to take diagnostic imaging of patients. They work with the Physician playing a vital role in patient care to read the results of an x-ray.

Qualities: Attentive, Collaborative

Yield Engineer: Yield engineers work closely with process engineers to improve product yield and troubleshoot process flow from root causes to equipment tuning.

Qualities: Communicative, Problem solver and Analytical Skills

Zoologist: Studies the origins, genetics, diseases, life progression, and behaviors of animals. They may devote their entire career to the study of one specific specie or group of species, or their work can be more generalized. Zoologists that work in zoos participate in the direct care of animals.

Qualities: Nature Lover, Critical thinker, Stamina, Emotional stability.

STEM CAREERS WORD SEARCH

P	H	D	H	K	R	B	L	S	T	F	T	L	R	T	J	S	Q	A	J	H	I	F	I	N	B	M	R	U	W
E	I	A	S	Q	O	I	R	K	Y	U	O	X	P	A	U	W	Y	N	D	W	Y	S	N	D	A	X	N	R	Z
E	S	O	N	A	Z	S	V	V	O	V	O	O	L	I	X	H	W	Q	R	X	D	Y	D	S	N	K	E	O	C
D	T	Q	Q	A	I	N	U	D	E	W	P	W	D	I	A	Y	U	T	C	P	K	E	U	L	L	G	U	L	S
X	O	F	Y	J	L	K	V	U	J	T	X	H	H	S	V	S	H	J	W	Y	S	L	S	W	Y	F	R	O	B
M	T	H	L	M	J	Y	J	G	N	M	E	U	A	W	C	I	E	W	K	Q	T	E	T	M	M	N	O	G	B
P	E	T	Z	P	Z	S	T	E	Q	K	I	R	M	R	X	I	E	G	V	M	R	G	R	W	O	A	L	I	E
Z	C	O	B	M	O	P	X	I	K	U	O	P	I	S	M	M	E	E	D	O	W	H	I	H	F	Q	O	S	M
L	H	O	T	L	O	G	R	S	C	M	W	P	C	N	G	A	P	N	F	W	E	L	A	R	L	O	G	T	B
E	N	I	S	G	L	N	A	P	B	A	F	W	H	U	A	Y	C	W	T	O	W	Q	L	W	H	D	I	G	M
D	O	M	V	E	O	W	Y	O	F	J	L	L	X	T	H	R	M	I	W	I	J	D	E	K	R	R	S	I	M
C	L	A	G	O	G	A	T	R	L	Q	V	C	W	D	H	R	I	J	S	K	S	Z	N	S	E	D	T	R	V
U	O	K	R	L	I	Z	E	T	A	T	U	V	H	E	I	A	Q	A	T	T	R	T	G	F	T	I	X	K	X
M	G	E	O	O	S	E	C	S	B	G	V	A	D	E	B	E	L	T	N	B	W	E	I	M	U	D	I	E	B
E	I	R	B	G	T	E	H	P	M	F	P	A	L	J	M	D	T	M	B	C	H	N	N	B	O	Y	B	C	W
D	S	W	O	I	C	B	N	H	A	U	I	C	N	I	A	I	E	I	O	H	J	U	E	Z	U	I	K	O	V
I	T	Q	T	S	B	N	O	Y	N	E	T	K	Y	K	T	V	S	V	T	L	S	B	E	L	Z	E	L	L	M
C	C	V	I	T	E	R	L	S	A	G	A	T	M	I	M	Y	A	T	E	I	O	D	R	D	I	L	J	O	L
A	I	H	C	D	E	Y	O	I	G	R	N	J	R	N	B	F	S	D	M	L	A	G	A	H	S	D	J	G	Z
L	U	O	E	Q	K	H	G	C	E	S	D	U	T	E	M	U	M	C	E	Q	O	N	I	V	U	E	O	I	C
W	B	V	N	T	E	G	I	I	R	A	E	V	D	S	V	D	X	K	I	V	B	P	O	S	N	N	S	S	D
R	V	C	G	K	E	N	S	A	J	I	C	W	G	I	L	Y	B	L	L	E	E	I	E	B	T	G	X	T	P
I	N	S	I	B	P	G	T	N	W	E	F	A	U	O	Z	I	S	P	U	B	N	L	U	R	E	I	R	L	Q
T	O	E	N	K	E	Y	T	D	T	J	I	Y	Y	L	U	D	G	V	V	G	W	T	O	D	I	N	V	O	R
E	I	A	E	I	R	K	B	N	G	D	B	B	L	O	H	P	G	T	N	A	S	O	I	P	L	E	G	Y	W
R	N	Y	E	I	H	O	N	X	L	Q	T	Z	E	G	Q	R	Q	J	N	I	L	M	O	S	E	E	Y	G	R
K	D	S	R	A	Q	R	U	S	H	U	M	C	Z	I	P	J	D	O	G	I	Z	A	F	T	T	R	V	P	M
X	N	H	U	Y	D	F	I	X	K	T	V	I	G	S	J	K	C	I	V	I	L	E	N	G	I	N	E	E	R
K	P	F	N	M	G	Q	P	Q	G	A	Z	C	F	T	I	Z	B	K	I	Z	H	A	V	J	R	T	J	V	L
N	U	X	I	V	G	A	K	W	S	T	S	X	I	N	R	N	F	Z	K	K	Z	K	H	M	T	P	E	Z	Y

AnalyticalChemist, Beekeeper, CivilEngineer, Dietitian, Ecologist, FoodScientist, Geologist
Histotechnologist, IndustrialEngineer, JavaDeveloper, Kinesiologist, LabManager,
MedicalWriter, Neurologist, Ophthalmologist, Pharmacist, QualityScientist,
RoboticEngineer, SportsPhysician, Toolmaker, Urologist, Veterinarian,
WebDeveloper, XrayTechnologist, YieldEngineer, Zoologist, Ecologist

Made in United States
Orlando, FL
02 June 2022